A Mixed Bag

SHARADA MURALIDHARAN

ISBN
Paperback 979-8-89699-996-6
Hardcase 979-8-89777-270-4

I would like to thank my friends and family who have been with me through this journey, and have helped me complete these poems!

My special thanks to my husband, who patiently read my poems and gave his review. I would like to thank my children and grandchildren for being my cheerleaders. Many thanks to my buddy Jaishree Srinivasan, her paintings have inspired me to write a few poems in this book. Truly appreciate my sister for her continuous encouragement and support.

I would like to dedicate this book to my parents who were my guiding light.

Sharada Murali

Contents

Retirement

Retirement

Retirement! Retirement!
What is Retirement anyway....?
Is it all work for no pay?
No one hears what we say....
Or, time to recline and lay?
Well, days go by, without a hey!
Join this privileged club if you may,
There's none to question your stay!
You are your boss all the way...
Friends and family will be at bay!
Retirement is not all joy and fun,
Will be days that are lonely and shun,
Tons of things need to get done,
It seems there's time for none.
Cheer up! Hi, retirees cheer up!!
Is this retirement...? What do you say....?

Deepawali

Let the Festivity and celebration begin!!
Light over darkness wins!
Knowledge over ignorance to prevail!
Darkness and obstacles to derail.

Diyas decorate every home,
People in the fineries happily roam.
Firecrackers illuminate the sky,
Flowerpots and Rockets zoom up high!

Friends and families exchange pleasantries,
Grand display of sweets and savories.
Booms and bangs surround,
Joy and happiness all around!!

A day to give and forgive,
A day to reflect and relive.
A day to pray for peace and tranquility,
A day to herald unity!!

Navarathiri

Nine nights of festivity!
Nine nights of divinity,
Nine nights of celebration,
Nine nights of jubilation!!

Dolls decked in rows!!
Groomed in fineries and bows.
We hear the holy bells ring!
Young ladies heartily dance and sing!!

Goddess sits on her mighty throne,
Her magnificence, brilliantly shown!
She lights the light of knowledge unknown
Removes ignorance, and ushers to the holy zone.

Let peace and prosperity unveil,
May the darkness set sail...
For happiness and joy to prevail!
Goddess thy mercy we hail!!

Thanksgiving

As the Thanksgiving day rolls around,
We nurture thoughts truly profound,
Friends and families love abound!
Sure, time to rejuvenate and rebound.

It's a day to count our blessings,
A day we share the spirit of giving,
A day to show what we prize and care,
A day of gratitude in the air!

Grateful for sun, that shines bright,
Grateful for stars at night,
Grateful for the heavenly light.
Grateful for the pure delight!

Let's forgive and forget our divide,
Spot light on triumphs with pride,
Pray for guidance, worries to tide,
Raise a toast with family by our side!!!

Yum yum yum!!!

Fun fair of biscotti in town,
Some are white, some are brown,
Carberry almond, is the crown,
All are yummy!! will never be a frown!!

Dry, crunchy, oblong in shape!!
Yummy, yum biscotti makes us sniff and gape!
Dunk them in a cup of chocolate,
It's savor no one would want to escape.

Found in plenty in sunny Tuscany,
Relish them with some tea and honey,
Flavor and varieties are so many!!
If you wait, you may not get any...!!

Coconut Grove

Coconut trees in their grove,
Stand tall and tanned as we rove,
Green fronds welcome as we drove,
Truly amazed by the treasure trove!

The climbers mount the trees in rhythm,
Secured to a rope, in style they scale them,
With skill and mastery to reach the green gem!
Let's celebrate their artistry with applause and drum(s)!

Times when our throats gets dry,
Trees offer its sweet nectar, ready to gratify!
Pure health drinks stored in piñata hang high!
Delicious heavenly juice, oh my…!

Trees grow majestic, green and tall,
To heed to the Lords heavenly call,
Palm leaves folds its arms to thank and pray,
For this glorious solemn day!

Christmas

Streets and homes dazzle in red and green,
Gold and silver stars glitter and glow in between,
Spruce decked up, twinkle and gleam,
Christmas carols have started to beam!

Season of happiness and giving begin,
Jubilation and cheer ring in,
Family and friends gather to chillin,
It's the time to celebrate with our kith and kin!

Holy star guided the three wise men to the shrine,
With gifts, they follow the sign,
To see the birth of the son of the divine!
Whose glory and grandeur will ever shine!!

Church bells chimes to honor the holy day!
Time has come to kneel and pray,
To the son of God in a manger, on a bed of hay,
For guidance, peace and serenity each day!

Seashells

Gathered these beauties by the shore!
Colors, shape, and size galore!
Washed ashore as the waves roar,
Scattered like pearls on the sandy floor!

So delicate! colors, pastel and warm,
Yet strong and mighty in form,
Lay on the shore tranquil and calm,
Oh! so magical to hold them in our palm!

Toss, turn, and twirl to the rhythm of the waves,
Meander through the darkest ocean caves,
Holds the mystic sound, as the waters lave,
In poise they move out of their safe enclave!!

A saunter by the white sandy shore,
Spruced up with beauties,so pure,
Couldn't ignore their charm and allure!
Picked a few stunners that washed ashore!

Power of Love!!

Love is divine, love is reverence,
Love is selfless, love is patience,
Love is devotion, love is forgiveness,
Love illuminates, love ends darkness.

Love is deference, love is immortal,
Love eludes hatred and violence,
Love fosters happiness and peace,
Love is liberty, love is freedom!

Love emanates from our spirit and soul,
Love opens up every mind and heart,
Love is pure worship and veneration,
Love blends Self with the Supreme!!

King of colors

Who are you with a brilliant hue….?
Magnificent orange and blue!
You are a flying jewel! It is true!
Where do you live? I have no clue..

Sharp, long, dagger like bill,
See you scanning down the hill,
Waiting to grab your kill?
Swooping for the catch, isn't it thrill?!

I hear no songs,just shrill flight calls,
You are Vibrant, gentle and small!
Makes a bystander enthrall!
Oh bird! you are serene,divine and all…!

Old age

Days and nights seem too slow,
All seems gray without a glow,
Heart seems drained and low,
Get spirited, we need to end the show!

No day goes by without a sigh,
Weeks and months don't seem to fly.
When is the time to bid goodbye..
The blue sky seems too far and high

The eyes are veiled with a sheer
The sounds around get unclear
Limbs buckle and become insecure
Soul ready to move without a spoor!

Glorious days lived are gone,
Still wait to see the tranquil dawn,
Give me lord the strength to live...
Reaching your abode, the task fulfilled!!

The brightest star!!

I see the brightest star in the sky!
Sparkling in peace, as we cry..
Divine twinkle, luminous glow,oh my!
Gracefully shining as days go by...

Lived a life of service,and care,
The angel's-loss we cannot bear,
A precious soul, so unique and rare,
Creator, you sure have been unfair.

Filled our lives with cheer and joy,
Day star's rise and set, you enjoyed!
Loved children, music, games,and all,
Dear star, keep shining as nights fall!

Mahatpadam

Glorious Blue lotus bloom!
Sacred,sublime, dispels all our gloom!
Showers us with ineffable boon,
Shields the macrocosm from doom!

Enchanting, mystic music in the air!
Creates joy, healing for all who care,
Divinity plays his sarang from a pier!
Mesmerized cosmos sets the stage on fire!

Magnificent melody, and glowing lights,
Awakens our spirit and soul to pure delight!
Guides us through the maze of illumination,
To reach the lotus feet for salvation!

A Masked woman!

Smile buries her hurts and tears,
This has been her for years.
Grins, hides her inner screams,
Mask she wears, pretends to beam!

Disguises sorrow, appears happy,
Many emotions concealed sadly.
Pretentious life, no one who cares,
Deep hurts, times difficult to bear.

Not a soul understands her.
She yearns to let loose, break free,
World just sees her masked cover.
She longs to show what's under.

She has a problem, is all she hears,
Her distress, needs a buddy to share,
Smiley mask she continues to wear,
Waiting on the world to be fair!

JANUARY
1
HAPPY
NEW
YEAR!

Holly jolly New Year!

Holly, jolly New Year!
Filled with nothing but cheer,
Dear ones always near,
Explore untouched frontier!

New stage, new acts, to premier!
Praying for the fogs to clear,
Start the journey as a pioneer,
Be blessed by the superior!

Follow dreams, nothing to fear!
Glory is going to be yours for sure!
Life's journey is for you to steer,
Buckle up for a glorious year!

Poinsettias

Red, pink, and white blooms,
Offsets the cold winter's gloom!
Flowers spread in a magical plume,
Rings in the holiday's boom!

Velvety poinsettias, red and green,
Seasonal blooms it's always been,
Silvery frost forms a glowing sheen,
Bright blossoms, in summers unseen!

Holiday festivity, bliss and delight in air,
Bright floral bracts pops everywhere,
Starry red flowers arrives each year,
Brings loads of joy and cheer!

????? ???????

Questions I often ask!
Who Am I? What is my task?
When do I hang up my mask?
How long will my act last?

Days and nights seem too long,
Heart has started its farewell song,
Hay days,and primetime bygone,
How long will this show prolong?

No hopes, or dreams left behind,
Vigor and fire not in my mind,
Life's deed performed and signed,
Lord! How long does this bond bind?

CHOICES

Choices

Infinite choices abound around us!
Opportunities and options amaze us,
Family and friends ground us,
Right choices, sure to direct us!

Sound decisions are for us to make,
Insights, and experiences we take,
Fear and indolence to forsake,
Endless possibilities open the gate!

Each day brings eternal choices,
It prompts us to make compromises,
Listen to your positive inner voices,
You are poised to share rejoices!

VIDYODAYA
MATRICULATION
HIGHER SECONDARY

Friends!

Fidus friends are hard to find,
Sincere,honest, and kind,
Echt, compassionate to bind,
Buddies to relax and unwind!

Friends are precious and dear,
They can see, hear and cheer!
Always ready to give a hand,
Have hearts that understand!

Friends adore you for who you are,
Watch and guide you from afar!
True friends don't bicker or spar,
Only make you feel like a superstar!!

Reflections!

Oh mirror on the wall,
You reflect us one and all!
Can you hear our inner call?
There's beauty within us all!

Clouds, you reflect sun, moon and stars,
Create Rainbows! oh how glorious you are!
The image you click glows above par
Your praise is sung near and far,

Water, you reflect the mighty sky,
Canvas you paint is a treat for the eye!
Still waters get printed in bright hues!
Moonlight shines as silvery dew!

Mind, reflects our highs and lows!
Aids to choose a path free of woes,
Maneuver through the life's maze,
Spell the truth, and clear the haze!

Super Trio

Found two gems after decade(s)
Friendship and bond never did fade!
Unity and amity harmoniously made,
Well-wishers, I can never trade!

Never regret calls that get chatty,
Laugh and giggle until teary!
Boosts spirit and soul when lonely,
Cheering adventure and journey!

Where were you all these years?
The best of the best peers!
Love and care immensely we share,
Let's celebrate this pact that's rare!

Ian

Hi monster, you left a path of destruction,
Created panic and disruption.
Swirled around smashing all obstructions,
Days, months, years for reconstruction..

Eerie silence before you arrived,
Came with a force and strength disguised.
Picked moisture, speed, and got energized.
Your fury and wrath left us paralyzed.

Power grids splintered, roofs tattered,
Windows shattered, tree limbs fractured,
Gust of wind whooshed, derbies scattered.
Rivers, lakes battered, Roads jiggered...

You charged up the coast like a Ram,
Destroying our peace and calm,
Brought life to a pause and jam...
Ian, why this fury? Why this bam?

Pure Symphony

Oh! what a colorful symphony,
Glows! shines in sync and harmony!
Hear the garden-dwellers melody?!
Scene, breadth taking,pure ecstasy!!

She flies in winds, a day hot or cold,
As cheery bright florets unfold!
Share her sweet stories untold!
Together they are radiant and bold!

Crimson rose opens its dainty wings,
Sits on red dahlia as it gently swings,
Sprinkles powdery dust she brings!
Delights on royal brew meant for kings!!

Galloping Away!

A dance so brilliant and upbeat!
As waves play their musical feat,
Hooves move in a synchronized beat,
Watching the scene is sure a treat!!

The saffron sky adds a golden glow,
A perfect setting for a splendid show!
Gentle breeze sets a tune as it blows,
Rhythm of life is ready to flow!

Horses reflect their heavenly dance,
As they move in a rhythmic prance!
Stallion and mare in a perky romance!
Take each heart and soul to a trance!

Lessons from the tempo of trotters' feet,
To love life, and make it sweet!
Follow the trail of spirit untamed,
Freedom follows the power reclaimed!

Tangerine Sheen

Eastern sky dazzles in copper glow,
Adore the brilliance of divine halo!
Flora in dark suites, gently bow,
Get ready to watch a grand show!

Bronze luster washes the night sky,
Morning star adds a glossy dye,
Golden shimmer stops all passerby,
What a mesmerizing beauty! Oh my!

Brass sky looks at the mirror below,
A meandering river gently flow,
Sailboat sails as warm winds blow,
Saffron scene! Gorgeous and mellow!!

Madonna Lilies

Oh so glorious! Bright and fair,
Stately lilies seen as happy pair,
Scent so delightful, fine and rare,
Freshness and serenity fills the air!!

White lilies symbol of love and purity,
Glows with peace and tranquility.
Trumpets seen in magnificent variety,
Epitome of nature's pure divinity!

Regal lilies spotted hand in hand,
In sheer bliss and repose they stand,
Clad in brilliant robes! simply grand,
Stage set for stars to play the band!

Dazzling Deity

Nine nights of dazzling celebration,
Display of vibrance, and exhilaration!
Festivities galore, in pure devotion,
Tradition cherished for generations!

Goddess worshipped in all fondness!
Destroyer of evil,heralds goodness,
Blesses all with grace and kindness,
It is time for revival and forgiveness!

Musical bands saturate the air,
Fragrant flowers bedecked with care,
Colorful lassies exhibit skill and flair,
Dazzling lights, light up the fun fair!

Tender Love

A tusker stands majestically tall,
Beside her walks an adorable doll,
Cow and calf seem to have a ball!
Trudging through the jungle, and all!

Backdrop so crisp, tranquil and fresh,
Can hear the melody of the thrush,
Puddles reflect the duo's mighty lush,
As they take a stroll, in no rush!

Baby enjoys mom's tender care,
Teaches her tricks to fend, and dare!
A divine mystical bond they share,
Mother's love has no compare!!

A Divine Scene!

Delicately crafted golden leaves!
Sensuous ,warm,gentle breeze!
Reflective puddle is sure a tease,
Stunning scene makes one freeze!

Wet street, paints the glossy sky,
Heavenly lamps stand tall and high!
Fall foliage dribbles down with a sigh,
Evergreens wishes them a hush goodbye.

A road less trekked bends winds ahead,
Dare the path few have dare to tread,
Fear and despair you are sure to shred,
Feel the divinity and bliss as it spreads!

Flower Girls

Fragrance of fresh cut flowers in air,
Lassies ready for the market fair!
Basket of blooms their heads bare,
Finest of florets picked with care.

Bouquet ready for a dear friend,
Choicest posies set as gifts to send,
Exquisite festoons to adorn your end!
Colorful lei to spread a Hawaiian trend!

Golden Shrine

Holy Shrine doused in gold,
Gilded dome, majestic an bold,
Divine light seems to enfold!
Sacred ground, a wonder to behold!

The pool of nectar reflects the glow!
Oh my what a magnificent show!
An abode of serenity stands tall,
An open house of worship for all!!

Kathak Dancer

Dancer moves in a mystical swing,
Hand gestures precise, enthralling!!
Feet taps to a rhythmic drumming!
Her twists and twirls, mesmerizing!

Exquisite expression of adoration!
Ankle bells evoke joy and jubilation!!
Her style and grace brings adulation,
A masterpiece of artistry in creation!

Damsel's eyes follows her graceful motion,
Her mind follows sincere devotion!
Dedication kindles her euphoric emotions,
Passion reflects in her blissful expressions!!